*A Kitten
on
Desire Street*

A Kitten on Desire Street

Barbara Peduzzi

Dear Gemma,

We hope you enjoy the book. —

Cousin Barbara
and Streetcar

The characters in the story, up until Raggedy is rescued, are fictional and any resemblance to persons living or dead is coincidental and unintentional. The events described in those parts of the story are fictional, but are based upon known facts, news reports and things described by rescuers in the affected areas. The people and incidents following his rescue are factual.

A Kitten on Desire Street
Copyright © 2010 by Barbara Peduzzi

All rights reserved.
No part of this book may be used or reproduced in any form, electronic or mechanical, including photocopying, recording, or scanning into any information storage and retrieval system, without written permission from the author except in the case of brief quotation embodied in critical articles and reviews.

Author photo by Jesse DeGroodt
Book design by The Troy Book Makers
Printed in the United States of America

The Troy Book Makers • Troy, New York
www.thetroybookmakers.com

To order additional copies of this title,
contact your favorite local bookstore or visit
www.tbmbooks.com

ISBN: 978-1-935534-79-2

Dedication

This book is dedicated to the people of Camp Katrina. What you did was absolutely amazing. My nine days there were one of the most phenomenal experiences of my life. It is also dedicated to all the people who put their work and their hearts into animal rescue everywhere. You make their world, and ours, better.

The first Camp Katrina sight was this sign by the road it was on - the port-a-potties did get moved after a while.

About This Story

When the people from NSAL came in the fancy bus to take rescued dogs and cats north to new homes, they had a cameraman making a video of the event. I showed them around the pens, and at each one he would shoot some footage and ask 'Now what's this animal's story?' Finally I told him 'They all have a story. We just don't know what it is.'

When I brought Streetcar home, I thought he should have a story, a history of his life before I knew him. This is what I imagine it might have been.

Special Thank You

A very special 'Thank You!' to Cassandra and Rita for hearing Streetcar meowing and rescuing him for me. Also thanks to Victoria Wright for editing and helping, to Judy and George and their reader for helpful tips, and to Naomi for staying up late and getting up early to read this and for saying 'this is the best book I ever read'.

All of the photographs in the book were taken by Camp Katrina rescuers, in and around New Orleans, and at Camp Katrina. These people saw things they will never forget; the pictures show only part of these. I thank them for their work, and for their photos: Chuck Meyer, Cassandra Koster, LuAnn Keyes, Lynne Clark – and if I missed anyone, I'm sorry, I thank you also.

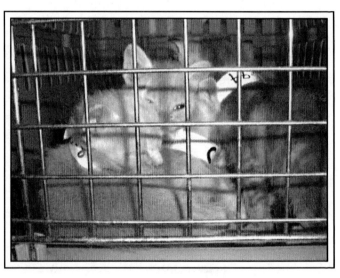

Pile of kittens, at Camp Katrina

CHAPTER 1

He was black and white, with a little white mustache and a ragged white stripe down his forehead. He had three sisters and a brother, and he was born in a box on the back porch of a small house on Desire Street in New Orleans.

"Momma, Momma, come look! Princess had kittens!" Shaneeka called her mother excitedly when she looked into the box and saw the just-born baby cats. They were so tiny they would fit into Shaneeka's cupped hands with room left over. Their eyes were tightly closed, their fur was still matted from the fluid they were in before they were born, their tails were skinny and short and their little ears could hardly be seen, flattened back against their heads.

"I know she did," her mother said. "Remember I told you she was ready to?"

"But I didn't think you meant today," Shaneeka answered.

"Well, when kittens – or anything else – are ready to be born, it doesn't matter what day it is or what's going on, they just get themselves born," her mother wisely told her. "Now leave her alone with them, we can't bother her too much right now."

"Can I pet them?" Shaneeka asked hopefully, as she watched the kittens wriggling about. They were too young and small to even stand up yet. They were making squeaky mewling noises and Princess was licking them and purring. She was quite pleased with herself and her new family. Two of the kittens were black and grey striped, with white on their tummies and feet. They looked a lot like Princess, who was what is called a tiger cat, she had the same stripes, white legs and a white mark from her nose to between her large eyes. One kitten was grey and one was all white.

"No. They're way too small to be petted. We can't touch them for a few days, until their eyes are open, and then just a tiny bit. Princess knows what to do, she'll take care of them."

"But how does she know?" the little girl wondered. "She hasn't had kittens before. Did you tell her what to do?"

Momma laughed and said, "Nope, I didn't have to. Animals just know, that's all. Come in the house and do your schoolwork – and there just might be a cookie in there."

"All right," Shaneeka nodded. She slowly turned away from the box and scuffed her feet as she reluctantly followed her mother, turning to look back at Princess and the kittens with every step. She did her school work, but she kept thinking about the kittens, and she ate the cookie, but she kept thinking about the kittens. Shaneeka thought they were the cutest things she had ever seen. She thought the black and white one was the very cutest of them all.

Maybe they were the cutest things she had ever seen. Shaneeka lived with her father and mother in New Orleans, in the part of town called the Ninth Ward. Their house was spotless, but small.

Shaneeka's house might have looked like this

Her father worked hard as a maintenance man at a big hotel downtown. Whenever anything needed to be fixed, the hotel people would tell him and he would do it, from changing light bulbs to repairing damaged furniture to cleaning carpets. He could fix almost anything and had to go up and down the many stairs in the tall hotel all day long to do all the things that were needed. He did not make much money, and her mother helped by doing housework for people, but she had not had much of it to do lately. She made up for it by keeping their house cleaner than ever, and by sewing Shaneeka's clothes and cooking lots of good food for them. There was not much left over for toys after they paid for the house and food and necessary things.

Shaneeka knew she was loved, though, and she passed some of that on to Princess. Now she could hardly wait to pass more of it on to her kittens.

When Shaneeka's father came home, her mother told him about their new little family. "Well, that's some news, all right," he said, "but what are we gonna do with five more cats? We can't get food for Princess some of the time."

"Now, you know I already found homes for some of them – that one family up on Elysian Fields that I clean for wants one, and the new minister…"

"Hmmph," was all that Shaneeka's father said.

"Shaneeka's so excited, I thought she'd pop right out of her skin when she saw them. Maybe we could keep just one for her to raise."

"Hmmph," Shaneeka's father said again.

Shaneeka woke up early the next morning and jumped out of bed. She raced right out to see Princess and her kittens. The kittens could move around a little bit, but they were still as tiny as they had been the day before. "When will they be big enough to pet and hold?" Shaneeka asked her mother.

"Not for a few more days. Now you get along to school."

Shaneeka told everyone at school about Princess's kittens. They all wanted to come and look at them, but Shaneeka said she would have to ask her mother first.

"Not until they are a little older," her mother said, "Princess would be nervous with a passel of giggling girls around her babies. Right now it's enough for her to let us near them. Tomorrow maybe we can try petting them a tiny bit ourselves, though."

Shaneeka did not know how her mother knew so much about cats and kittens, but she decided she should do what her mother said. The next day she woke up even earlier and ran to the kitchen. "Can I pet the kittens today, Momma?" she asked.

"Well, let's go see if Princess thinks we can," her mother answered. They went out to the back porch and knelt down by the box with the little family in it. "What do you think, Princess? Can this pesky little girl touch your babies?"

Princess looked at Shaneeka and her mother and gave a quiet "Meow."

"I think she said we can, Momma," Shaneeka said.

"Let's try." Her mother slowly reached into the box and touched Princess's head, and then stroked her ears and neck and back, while Princess purred and curled around her kittens. Then Momma touched each of the kittens very gently and lightly, while Princess watched closely.

"Now you try it," Momma told Shaneeka, "very slowly and gently."

Shaneeka moved her hand as slowly as she could, and touched Princess very softly. Princess purred, so Shaneeka touched each of the kittens very, very gently. Princess twitched her ears but just watched to see that Shaneeka treated her babies right. "They're so little and so soft!" Shaneeka exclaimed. She touched each one of them, but she touched her favorite, the black and white one, just a little bit longer.

Time to be petted, St. Bernard Parish shelter

"They'll get bigger soon enough. Kittens don't stay kittens long," her mother said, "You being just a little kitten of a girl yourself have to get to school now." So Shaneeka went to school, even though she would rather have stayed home and watched Princess and the kittens all day.

Shaneeka and her mother petted Princess and the kittens a little bit more every day. After what seemed to Shaneeka to be the very longest time ever, her mother said, "I think you could hold one of them for a little bit, if you'd like." Shaneeka could not say a word, she just gasped and then looked into the box to see which one to hold first.

The kittens' eyes were starting to open now. As Shaneeka looked at them in the box, the little black and white one gazed back at her and mewed. "That one, Momma, I want to hold the black and white one," she said. Her mother picked the kitten up and handed it to Shaneeka, who thought she could just burst with excitement.

"Now hold it loosely," her mother told her. "Don't squeeze it. Kittens are just babies, and they're still fragile. You could hurt one without even meaning to."

"I would never hurt one of Princess's kittens, Momma," Shaneeka said, as she held the little kitten close to her chin. He looked at her again, and wriggled around until his tiny paws were on each side of her neck and then he stretched his head up and touched her chin with his nose. "It kissed me, Momma! Did you see that? The kitten kissed me."

Shaneeka's mother chuckled, "Yes, I saw that, but I think maybe it's looking to see if it can get anything to eat from you. That's enough holding, put him back down now. You can do it again tomorrow."

"All right," Shaneeka said. "I want to keep that one, Momma. Can I, please? Can I? He likes me. He kissed me."

"We'll see," was all Momma would say. Later that night, though, she talked to Shaneeka's father. "Shaneeka wants to keep one of those kittens."

"Hmmph," he grumbled. "All I can do to put food on the table for people, never mind for cats."

"Well, now, you know they don't eat much. Princess is the best mouser in the neighborhood, and she's bound to teach her kitten that."

"Yes, she is," said Shaneeka's father. He put his hand down to stroke Princess, who just happened to have come in to the room when her name was mentioned. The kittens were big enough to be left alone for a short time now, she had decided. So Princess got a petting, even though Shaneeka's father tried to keep her mother from seeing it.

"I told her we'd see. Remember I told you about folks that might want some?" Momma was quiet for a moment, and then added, "She surely does like that little black and white one, though."

"Humph," Shaneeka's father grunted again.

Every day, Shaneeka was able to hold the kittens for a little bit longer. She held all of them, and played with all of them, but the little black and white one was her favorite. By now, school was over for the summer, and she was home all day. She and the kittens went into their small back yard and played. She would sit and pet them, and let them climb on her, and wave a string back and forth over their heads so they could try to catch it. When they got tired from playing and fell asleep in the sun she would just sit and watch them.

One day, some people drove up in front of Shaneeka's house. Her mother hurried out to the street to meet them, and brought them to the back yard. "Shaneeka, honey, these are the Adamses. They would like to have one of Princess's kittens." There was a woman and two little girls, one bigger than Shaneeka and one smaller. Shaneeka stepped back, and the kittens scrambled over to the new people to sniff and see what they were. The little girls giggled at how the kittens ran. One tiger-striped kitten went to the bigger girl and one went to the smaller girl. Each girl reached down and picked a kitten up and said at the same time, "I want this one, Mommy!"

"Oh, dear," their mother said, "Which one gets which kitten?"

"Well, now, I don't know what to tell you," Shaneeka's momma said, "but it sure would be a shame to disappoint either one of your little girls."

The girls' mother looked at her children with their kittens and sighed, "Oh, well, they're small – for now! All right. You each can have one."

"Hooray!" the girls cheered, hugging their kittens. "Thank you," they both said. Shaneeka and her mother said goodbye to the tiger-striped kittens. Shaneeka felt a little bit sad to see the two kittens go, but she was also very glad that the girls had not picked the black and white kitten that she hoped she could keep for her own. She loved Princess, but there was something special about this little kitten who had been the first one she held and who had kissed her that day.

The next Sunday after church, Shaneeka's mother stopped and talked to the minister. "Those kittens are getting to be a good size now," she said, "Two of them already went to live up in Elysian Fields, and the rest of them could go to a new home any time."

What the floods left of what might have been the church the family went to

"How about if I come by later today?" the minister asked. "I'll bring the family to see which one they want."

That afternoon the minister, his wife and their children came to Shaneeka's house. Her mother offered them iced tea and a seat in the parlor, but they said they wanted to see the kittens, so they all went to the back yard. They looked at all of them, but the white kitten kept going to the minister and mewing at him. "I do believe this white kitten is trying to tell me something," he said. "What would be more fitting to live in a minister's house than a pure white kitten?" So the white kitten went to live in the parsonage.

When the people left with that kitten, Princess went down the sidewalk after them, and sat there a long time looking in the direction they had gone with her baby.

When she finally went back to the two kittens that were left, Shaneeka noticed that Princess seemed to be staying closer to them. "Does Princess miss her babies?" Shaneeka asked her mother.

"Not really, not for very long, anyway. Animals are like that. They know they can't keep all their babies around them forever. Just like people know some day their babies are gonna grow up and leave them."

Shaneeka ran and hugged her mother. "I won't leave you, Momma," she said.

"Well, now, someday you will, but it won't be for quite a while yet," her momma smiled.

The two kittens that were left played with each other, and with Shaneeka. One day, Shaneeka and Momma went to the grocery store. When the grocer was ringing up their things, he said, "Say, didn't I hear that the minister got a kitten from you folks?"

"Yes, he did," Momma said. "Our Princess had five babies. There's two left. Do you need a cat?"

"Now you know I just might," he answered. "You know, with this food around I sure do get some mice in here, and a cat to catch them would be just the thing. I had that big gray tom cat, but he got old and he just disappeared a little while back. I think he went to the big mouse hunt in the sky, if you get my drift."

Shaneeka thought she did get his drift, even though she knew he had been talking in 'grown-up' to try to keep her from understanding what he said.

"Well, we just happen to have a gray kitten," her momma said. "He's already a pretty good size, and Princess is a great mouser, so he should have some of that in him."

"I might just be interested," the grocer nodded. "Maybe I will stop by when I close the store and look him over." He did exactly that. "You look like you are going to grow up to be strong and fast," he told the kitten, "and that's just what I need to keep the mice out of my store." The kitten just mewed, but he seemed happy enough to be going with the grocer.

Shaneeka stroked the black and white kitten. He was the only one left. She took a deep breath before she asked, "Momma, can we keep this one? Please?"

"We'll see," her mother said. "You know we don't have a lot extra to feed even a little kitten and he's going to grow and need more to eat. If someone comes looking for him, then so be it – but if no one does, he is meant to stay with us."

The afternoon was hot, without even a breeze. Shaneeka's parents sat on the back steps, watching the kitten play with a piece of paper Shaneeka had crumpled up and thrown to him. He batted at it with his paws and ran away when it skittered across the grass. Then he sneaked up on it and rolled over with it in his paws, biting at it. Princess thought that since she was a mother she was too old to play like that and sat on the steps next to Poppa.

"Why does he chase the paper like that?" Shaneeka asked.

"That's how kittens learn to hunt," her mother said. She fanned herself. "He practices by chasing things."

"Look how fast he is," Shaneeka pointed. "He'll be a good hunter, then, won't he?"

"Yeah, but he's got some raggedy markings on him," her father observed. "Look at his face – it doesn't know if it wants to have a white mustache or a black beard."

"He's pulled that paper raggedy, that's for sure," her mother said.

"Raggedy! His name can be Raggedy!" Shaneeka cried. She was very excited, because she had been trying to think of just the right name for the kitten.

"Raggedy? Well, I guess that works," Shaneeka's mother nodded. And that seemed to settle the matter. The kitten would stay with them!

Shaneeka's father just said, "Humph. Raggedy. Some name for a cat." The kitten came up beside him and he turned to hide his smile as he reached down to scratch the top of its head. "I guess we got us another cat." He pretended to be gruff, but he knew how much Shaneeka loved the little cat.

Raggedy knew they were talking about him

Shaneeka thought she would just overflow with happiness. She jumped up and hugged her mother and her father as hard as she could. "Oh, thank you! He won't eat much, I promise, and I'll take care of him and teach him how to behave and…and…." and she ran out of things to say, but she hugged her parents again, and then scooped Raggedy up and hugged him. "You're my kitten, Raggedy!" she whispered. "We'll have the best time together. You're going to be the handsomest, fastest, smartest, bravest cat ever."

Shaneeka was true to her word. She started right away teaching Raggedy things he would need to know to be a proper grownup cat, and he learned everything she taught him very quickly.

Princess was teaching Raggedy things at the same time. She taught him how to wash himself, even behind his ears and between his toes, and told him that washing was very important to cats.

Shaneeka slid a little box into the corner of their bathroom and put sand in it. "Here, Raggedy," said Shaneeka as she plopped the kitten into the box. "This is your inside bathroom place." Princess taught him how to scuff the sand over what he did in it, just as he did outside. Cats had always done that, even out in the wild, because it covered up traces of where they had been so that bigger animals could not track them as easily.

Shaneeka showed him where the food dish was. Some days they had cat food, and some days it just held scraps from dinner. Raggedy ate everything Shaneeka gave him. Princess taught him how to hunt mice so that, no matter what, he would be able to feed himself.

Princess taught him to watch for cars in the streets, and to look people over carefully to figure out if they were going to be nice or try to hurt him. She taught him that he should never try to go into any space where his whiskers touched the sides, because that meant his head and body would not fit there and he'd get stuck. And she taught him that his human family was very special (Raggedy thought, I already *know* that!) and that he should always try to make his person pleased with him and proud of him. Raggedy tried to remember everything Princess taught him, because he wanted his mother to be pleased with him and proud of him, too.

Shaneeka thought that her life could not possibly be any better. Raggedy was just as cute as he could be, and he was learning and growing every day. He would run around their yard and play, jumping up on the porch railing, and then leaping off to run around the yard again. Shaneeka would laugh and laugh at him. When he was tired of running and jumping, he would come and sit in her lap, and then he would climb up to put his paws around her neck and his chin on her shoulder and start to purr. Shaneeka loved those times most of all. Sometimes he would even put his little nose right in her ear and purr and purr. Shaneeka would laugh and push him away because that tickled! Raggedy would sigh because he was so contented.

CHAPTER 2

It was time for school to start again. She saw some of her friends during the summer, but she felt both sad and glad to be going back to school. She was excited to be in a new grade, and to be able to tell all her friends about Raggedy, but she was sad that she would not be able to spend all her time with him.

The night before school started, Shaneeka's father came home from work looking worried. "Have you heard any news today?" he asked her mother. "There's talk of a big storm that might come into the Gulf."

New Orleans, where Shaneeka and her family and Raggedy and Princess lived, was on the Gulf of Mexico. Sometimes big hurricanes came near their city, and there was hard rain and strong winds that damaged homes. That night her parents watched the news on their small, old television. The storm was a hurricane and it was named Katrina.

Shaneeka, safe in her bed, could hear her parents' worried voices. "Yes, indeed," her father said, "that sure looks like it might come right to New Orleans."

"Well," said Shaneeka's mother, "there's nothing we can do about the weather except wait for it to happen. We can do our best to board up the house and have supplies, but that's all we can do."

For the next few days, everyone in the city watched the news closely to see what this storm was doing. It was getting stronger and stronger. Hurricanes are measured in categories, and this one soon became a Category 5, the strongest storm. Everyone in the city worried about what the storm would do.

"It's headed right at us." Shaneeka's father said as he and her mother nailed boards that they found across their windows. "It's a big one, too."

The mayor was on the television and radio, telling people to evacuate. "Hmmph!!" Shaneeka's father said. "How are we going to evacuate, with no car to do it in and no buses coming around to take us out? Folks like us just have to ride it out."

Shaneeka and her mother made several trips to the store and got as much extra water and food as they could afford.

"If the hurricane comes, what about Raggedy and Princess?" Shaneeka asked. She slipped a big bag of cat food into the cart. Her mother noticed, but didn't tell Shaneeka to put it back. "If we evacuate, can we take them with us?"

"We'll bring them inside," her mother answered. "That's all we can do. If we're all right, they will be. From what I can tell, it's not *if* the hurricane comes, it's *when* it comes."

The hurricane came the next morning. Rain poured down, and the wind howled around their little house, and all the houses in their neighborhood. Shaneeka's family huddled inside, away from windows. Shaneeka clutched Raggedy to her, and her mother held Princess, who kept meowing and looking nervous. It seemed to Shaneeka and the frightened cats that the storm went on forever.

Finally, it seemed to stop. The sky was brighter,

and Shaneeka didn't have to shout to be heard. "It's over! Can I go outside?" She ran to the door and peeked outside. The whole street looked like someone had dumped a giant trash can all over it.

"No, you stay here with us," her father said. "That's only the eye – it'll be back as strong as before." He drew her a rough picture of the swirling storm, and pointed to the hole in the middle. It did look like an eye.

And then suddenly, it was back, and it sounded louder and fiercer than before. In spite of the rain and wind and noise and being afraid, Shaneeka finally fell asleep, with her head in her mother's lap. Raggedy went to sleep, too, with his paws around her neck.

When the storm finally moved away, they went outside. Their neighbors were outside, too, looking at the damage. Many houses had pieces of their roofs missing. There were limbs from trees on the streets and big puddles of water everywhere. Some people had not put boards on the windows and the glass had broken. Their houses were all wet inside.

It was a beautiful day. The whole neighborhood

was outdoors. Shaneeka's mother and father cleaned up their own yard and then helped their neighbors.

There was no electricity because of the storm, so they could not watch their television. A neighbor had a radio that ran on batteries, and told them the news of the towns that were swept away by the wind and waves of the storm. "Be thankful," people were saying, "the worst part missed us. But those poor people over in Mississippi, they lost everything. Pray for them, poor souls." Everybody thought they were out of the danger of the storm.

That night when she went to bed, Shaneeka prayed for the people who had been hurt by the storm, and said a thank you that her house did not have too much damage and that her family and Raggedy and Princess were all right. And she went to sleep, with Raggedy curled up on the pillow next to her.

CHAPTER 3

It was still dark outside when a loud noise suddenly woke Shaneeka up. Someone was pounding on their door and shouting. "The levee's broke!! Get up!! Get out!!"

Shaneeka was scared and called, "Momma!" as she started to get out of bed. Her father pushed open the door of her room and her mother was right behind him.

"Hurry, child – put some clothes on," her mother said quickly. She pulled some clothes out of the dresser and threw them to Shaneeka. Shaneeka was still not all the way awake, and she had trouble putting things on. Part of the trouble was that Raggedy, who had been sleeping with her, was scared, too. He was clinging to her and his little claws were digging into her skin.

"Get that cat out of the way!" her father shouted. He reached over, pulled Raggedy off Shaneeka's shoulder, and tossed him onto the bed.

"No, Poppa!" Shaneeka cried, and reached for her kitten.

"Shaneeka, we have to get out – there's a flood – we have to leave right now!" her mother urged.

"But I have to bring Raggedy!" Shaneeka cried and she clutched the kitten to her chest.

Shaneeka's father picked her up and carried her into the kitchen. There was already water on the floor of their house. Meowing loudly, Princess was standing on the kitchen table — something she would never have done normally, but she was afraid of the water. Shaneeka's mother never even chased her off.

"Hold on to the child, I don't know what's gonna happen when I open the door," her father said, as he reached for the back doorknob. Shaneeka's mother held her tightly and he opened the door. More water rushed in. Even though her mother was holding her high up, Shaneeka's feet were getting wet.

Flooded streets

"Come on!" her father yelled, "We have to get up on the roof!" He pulled her mother outside onto the back porch. The water was above the steps, and almost up to the railing. "Climb up on the rail and I'll push you up," he said. Shaneeka's mother did, with her father holding them both steady. Momma shoved Shaneeka up onto the roof, and with Poppa pushing her legs and feet, Momma was able to scramble up herself. Then her father grabbed the edge of the roof and slowly pulled himself up.

People were screaming and shouting. Everywhere

they looked, there was swirling water, covering the lawns and streets and rushing into the houses. Cars and toys were floating in it. Shaneeka was very scared and she started to cry. She held Raggedy tightly and they both shivered. "Where is Princess?" Shaneeka suddenly asked, "Did Princess get out of the house? She should be here with us! Momma, where's Princess?" Panicked, she started to move towards the edge of the roof, but her mother pulled her back.

"Don't go near the edge! Princess is smart. She'll take care of herself. We need to figure out what we're going to do now."

"Well, unless we can make a boat, I don't see that there's much we can do until help comes along," her father said. He stood up and looked around. All around them the water was getting deeper and deeper. "If this water doesn't stop, we may have to find out what we can do way too soon." He looked in every direction, trying to see what they could do if the water got to be higher than the roof of their house.

Shaneeka sat down and hugged Raggedy, and her mother put her arm around them both. "I wish that Princess had gotten out of the house," Shaneeka sobbed.

"Now don't you be giving up on Princess just yet," her mother said, although she was not sure she believed her own self.

The water had risen so fast, and Princess was, after all, an animal, and might not be able to figure out what was happening. Momma sighed and looked at the water. Then she looked again, at something that seemed to be moving in it, near the side of their house. "Oh, my!" she said, and moved closer to the place where she saw it.

It was Princess! She had gotten out of the house through an open window and she was trying to swim to the roof. The current of the water was so strong and fast that it kept taking her farther and farther away. She meowed loudly.

"What's that!" Shaneeka said, looking towards where the meow had come from. "It's Princess! Poppa, Momma, it's Princess – get her, get her!" she cried, and tried to stand up and go towards the swimming cat.

"No! Shaneeka, don't!" her mother shouted, pulling her back down. "Let your father try." He did, but Princess had been swept too far away from the house to reach.

Shaneeka started to cry again, "No! No, Raggedy can't lose his momma!" They watched, helpless, as the cat was dragged away by the strong water. Suddenly, she got caught in a swirl of it that was close to a tall tree that stood next to the street. Princess spun all the way around and then she reached out and grabbed the tree with her claws. For a scary moment, it looked like she might not be able to hang on, but then she pulled herself out of the water one paw at a time and clung to a branch. "Meow!" Princess yowled, looking back at her home and family.

"Poppa, go get her, please," Shaneeka begged. But deep down, she knew that he could not.

"No, we can't do that right now," he answered. "When the water goes down, she'll be able to get down by herself, and come home."

"Home," Shaneeka's momma sighed, looking down at the water. "We won't have much home left after this." And they all were quiet, because this was the first time they had thought about that. Everything they had was in their little house, and now it was completely under the dirty, rushing water.

"Poppa, how long will the water be this deep?" Shaneeka asked.

"I don't know," he answered truthfully. The flood was beyond anything that anyone had ever experienced, or even imagined. They could see other people on their roofs now. Some of them had a few things from their houses with them, and some others had dogs and cats, but most had only themselves.

The water had almost stopped growing deeper, but it was swirling around all the houses and trees and signs and poles. Things were floating in it, too – little things like a child's wagon, and lawn chairs, and even big things like cars!

Raggedy mewed and wriggled in Shaneeka's arms. "No, you can't get down and play, and there's no food – you'll just have to wait like we do," she said firmly. He mewed again, louder, and this time Princess heard him and meowed back. He looked across the water at her and mewed once more, very sadly. Princess meowed once more, too, and then settled down on a fairly wide branch of the tree and began to wash herself.

"See," Momma said, "Princess knows what to

do – wait and have a wash-up."

Shaneeka's father said, "Well, we surely will have to wait – but I don't know that I'd want to wash up in that." He pointed to the water. It was very dirty. It was an ugly dark color that was almost brown, and almost black and almost gray, like all three of them mixed together.

"What will we do, Poppa?" Shaneeka asked.

"I don't know," he answered. "Just wait and see what we can do, I guess."

"Well, I'm glad we're all safe, and Raggedy, too," Shaneeka said, "but I wish Princess was over here with us." And she hugged Raggedy hard. It seemed like Princess had told him he had to behave and wait, because he was very still and quiet.

They were all still and quiet. Poppa called out to a neighbor, who told him that their family was all right, and they were just waiting, too.

"How long you suppose they goin' to leave us here?" the neighbor asked Poppa.

"Hmmph! Mighty hard to say, I guess," he answered. "Don't know how they figure to get out here to help us – if they didn't get buses to take us away, don't know how they gonna get boats to rescue us. We just have to hang on until they do."

"Well, I hope everyone can," the neighbor said. They stopped talking and stood on their roofs and looked out over the flooded city.

As far as they could see, everything was covered with water. They could see the taller buildings of the downtown, and some of the overpasses of the freeway, and those were above the water, but those and rooftops were the only things. There were no cars and no people moving – just the ones on their rooftops.

The sun climbed higher in the sky and soon it was very hot on the roof. Shaneeka squirmed a little bit, but she knew better than to say anything. There was nothing to be done about it. Sometimes they got up and walked along the roof for a little bit, but mostly they just sat there, waiting.

A roof where people waited for help

Shaneeka kept hold of Raggedy because she was afraid he might jump or fall off the roof if she let him go. He got wriggly after a while, though. He was too active a kitten to be held for that long a time, no matter that they were sitting on the roof! Momma saw him trying to get down. "Why don't we sit together and make a fence with our arms and legs," she suggested. "That way he can move around a little bit but we can keep him with us."

"Do you think we can keep him from getting away?" Shaneeka asked.

"I think so," Momma answered. "If he does get out of our fence, where can he go? He'll come back to you to be held."

So they carefully moved around, and held their limbs to make a small closed in space between them, not quite as high as the top of Raggedy's back. Shaneeka let him go and he walked around, sniffing. Then he tried to jump and run a little bit, but there was not much space for that, because Shaneeka's arms were pretty short. "Poppa, can you do this?" she asked. "It would make a bigger space for Raggedy to play."

"Hmmph!" said Poppa. "All I got to do right now is make a space for a kitten to play!"

"Well," Momma pointed out, "it's not like you have a whole lot else happening right now."

Poppa didn't say anything to that, but he did come over and sit near Shaneeka and put his arms out around where Raggedy was. "Oh, that's bigger!" Shaneeka said, "He can almost run in here." Raggedy did for about two steps, just to show that he really could.

Shaneeka wiggled her fingers in front of him and

he chased her hand around the circle her parents' arms and legs made. She giggled at him jumping after her fingers.

"He's so funny, no matter what he does." She looked at her mother as she spoke. She fluttered her fingers and Raggedy jumped up after them – and landed outside her parents' arm fence! He looked around and, realizing he was free, he jumped again and ran down the roof.

"Raggedy, *no*!" Shaneeka screamed and leaped up to chase him. He thought it was a game and ran up and over the peak to the other side of the roof. Shaneeka tried to follow him, but she could not run on the slippery roof like he could. Her parents struggled to stand up and follow her.

"Sit *down*, girl!" her father commanded.

"Shaneeka, don't run after him – let him come back to you," her mother said. But Shaneeka was so frightened that something would happen to Raggedy that she didn't listen. She was scrambling to get to the other side of the roof to catch him, and Poppa was trying to catch up with her and stop her. Just then Raggedy scampered back to their side of the roof.

"Raggedy, come back!" Shaneeka called to him. "Come here!" She tried to grab him. Startled, the little kitten jumped away. He wasn't watching where he jumped to, though and he jumped too near to the edge of the roof. One of his feet slipped right off it onto nothing but air. Shaneeka saw this and reached for him, but she was too far away. "*Raggedy*! Noooo!" She screamed.

Raggedy tried to dig his little claws in, but his other feet slid down the roof. They heard a small splash in the water as Raggedy fell off the roof.

"Noooo!" Shaneeka screamed again. She threw herself towards where Raggedy had fallen, but she lost her balance and fell. The next thing the family knew, she was rolling down the slope of their roof towards the water.

"Shaneeka!" It was her mother's turn to scream.

There was a bigger splash. Shaneeka had fallen off the roof, too! She grabbed the very edge of it.

"Hang on, Honey, hang on!" her mother shouted. She inched towards where Shaneeka was clinging to the shingles.

Her father was closer, though, and he half-ran,

half-slid to where she was dangling in the water. "Don't move," he said, as she kicked to try to get out of the water and back onto the roof. He sat down and leaned over the side. "I'm going to grab your wrists and pull you up." He grasped Shaneeka's little wrists in his big hands. "Don't you do anything, don't move, so I don't lose hold of you."

Poppa pulled like he had never pulled anything before. He wriggled himself backwards up the roof as he dragged her out of the water, and even though Shaneeka was not very big yet, it took all of his strength to do those things and still hold her. The oily water made her skin very slippery.

Momma was near them by this time. She reached over and took one of Shaneeka's arms, and together they were able to pull her all the way back onto the roof with them. Momma grabbed Shaneeka and squeezed her as tightly as she could. "Oh, Shaneeka!" she cried, "Oh, Shaneeka. Oh, Shaneeka." That was all she could say, and then she had to stop saying it because she was crying.

Poppa just took them both in his big strong arms, and the family sat there on the roof while Momma cried and Poppa said something very softly that might have been "Hmmph," and sniffed, more than once. Shaneeka just shivered.

Suddenly she stiffened in her parents' grasp. "Raggedy! What about Raggedy?" she exclaimed.

Poppa and Momma looked at each other over Shaneeka's head. They had been so worried about her that they had forgotten about the kitten. It was plain on both faces that they did not think there was much chance the tiny kitten would survive in the deep, dirty water. Momma stroked Shaneeka's head and told her, "We'll look, child, but you mustn't get your hopes up. He's still very small and the water is very deep."

"No, Momma, don't say that," Shaneeka wept. "If something happens to him, it's my fault." She couldn't talk any more because she was crying so hard.

Poppa said, "I'll look for him."

Shaneeka just nodded, and buried her face against her mother.

So Poppa slid down to where he could see over the edge of the roof. He looked straight down to where Raggedy had fallen into the water and he did not see anything. He looked back and forth and then farther away from the house, even though he did not think a cat, especially one so small, could swim in that water. "Well, I'll be hog-tied!" he shouted. "Come here and look!"

Momma nudged Shaneeka and helped her towards Poppa. At first they could not see anything, but when he pointed, they saw the tiny black head with the ragged white stripe moving through the water. The only trouble was that it was moving away from their house. Small noises were coming from it, though, very small but determined *mews*.

"Raggedy – Raggedy, come back!" Shaneeka called, but he did not turn back.

Then they heard another *meow*. Princess was still in the tree, and she was looking right at Raggedy. Her tail twitched back and forth. Raggedy was trying his hardest, but it was a long ways to the tree, and his head was moving more and more slowly. Princess could see that her kitten was exhausted.

All of a sudden she meowed very loudly and jumped into the water. A 'V' spread in the water behind her as she swam to Raggedy. He had almost stopped moving when she touched his nose with hers. Then she swam past him, turned around, and put her shoulder behind Raggedy. She started swimming back to the tree.

"No, Princess, come this way, come back to us," Shaneeka cried. "Why won't she come to us?"

"She might know more than we do – she might know that he's too tired to swim all the way back here," Momma said.

They watched the two cats and felt very helpless. Shaneeka almost couldn't breathe, she was so afraid for Raggedy. "Oh, please, oh, please, oh, please," she whispered.

The water was swirling, and the wind was making little waves. Princess struggled on, though, still pushing her kitten. Once he slid, and she had to stop swimming forward and turn herself to get behind him again. Shaneeka gasped and held her breath until Princess was pushing him again. They moved a bit faster after that and soon were at the tree.

Princess pushed Raggedy until he put his claws into the tree trunk and held on, and then she grabbed it and pulled herself onto the first limb she could reach. She stretched down and grabbed Raggedy by the back of his neck with her teeth and tugged. With her pulling and him climbing, they were soon both sitting on the branch, panting.

"I know just how that cat feels!" Poppa said, and he put his arm around Shaneeka.

"So do I," said Momma, and put her arm around on the other side.

Shaneeka looked at each of her parents and sighed. "But what about Raggedy? How will we get him back?"

"I don't know," answered her mother. "But for right now he's safe with his own momma. She'll look after him, and you can see how they're doing."

"Nothing we can do – we got enough to look after ourselves right now," agreed her father.

They gazed over the water at the two cats in the tree. But they were all thinking different things. Shaneeka's father kept looking all around them to see if there was anything happening that might mean they could be rescued. Her mother was thinking that she was glad they were all safely together again.

But it was Shaneeka who said what they all had been thinking. "I sure wish we had brought some food when we got out of the house!"

"Mmm-hmm, and a nice cold lemonade," her mother agreed.

"Hmmph," was all her father said about it.

Finally, the sun started going down and it was cooler. It had been an exhausting day. Shaneeka tried to find a comfortable way to lie down on the roof. She finally stayed on her back, with Momma on one side and Poppa on the other. As she went to sleep, she heard her parents talking in low voices about what might happen.

It was not quite all the way light when Shaneeka woke up. She stretched and yawned. "I'm hungry – and thirsty."

Her mother said, "I know you are, honey, and so are we. But there's nothing to be done about it."

Shaneeka peered through the dim light. "Raggedy! Princess!" she called. "I don't see them!"

"Shhh," her father whispered. "Listen!"

Shaneeka could hear two faint voices, one saying "Meow!" and one saying "Mew, mew."

"They're there!" she said with relief. "I bet they're hungry and thirsty, too."

"I bet they are, but they'll be all right for a while more," Momma assured her, "just like us."

The big, hot sun came all the way up soon enough, and Shaneeka looked at the tree again. At first she couldn't see Raggedy and was frightened, but then when she looked more she could see that Princess curled on the limb, keeping him between herself and the tree trunk. Shaneeka sat on the roof, wrapped her arms around her knees, put her chin down on them and watched the cats. Before long, Raggedy woke up and stood, a little wobbly. "Hi, Raggedy," Shaneeka called, and he walked along the limb towards her. Princess followed him and tapped him with her paw.

"I don't know that I'd talk to him," Momma cautioned her, watching the girl and the cats. "He might decide to try to come to you. Princess will take care of him."

"I'm not going to stop watching them, though," Shaneeka said, and she wriggled into as comfortable a position as she could find.

All day they sat on the roof, watching the water and the cats and the other people. Some people were calling, "Help!" but there was no one to hear them. Shaneeka grew hungrier and thirstier and more worried about Raggedy and Princess.

"Listen!" Poppa suddenly said. "You hear that?" He stood up and turned towards a faint buzzing sound. "I think I hear a boat!"

Sure enough, they could hear what sounded like a motor boat. As the noise grew steadily louder, Shaneeka saw people jumping to their feet, waving from the rooftops. "Over here!" people shouted. "Help us!"

And then they saw the boats, coming right up where the street should be. One approached their roof. The man in it slowed the motor and shouted, "Are you people all right? Is anyone old, or sick here?"

"No, we're thirsty but we're all right," Momma said.

"We'll be back, then," the man said, "We want to get the ones who need it most out first." The boat sped off with a roar. It went near the tree where Princess and Raggedy sat. Princess just watched, but Raggedy was terrified. He raced up to the top of the tree.

"Raggedy, don't do that! You'll fall!" Shaneeka called to him. He turned and looked at her, and then looked down and mewed very loudly. He was a little scared, because now he could see how high he had scrambled. Princess meowed back to him, and then climbed a little ways towards him, meowing again. He looked at her, and slowly crept back down the tree trunk, hanging on as hard as his little claws could cling. It took a long time, and once he slid and Shaneeka's heart felt like it jumped right up to her throat, but he got back to the big branch where Princess was. She meowed loudly, as if she was scolding him, but then she washed the top of his head so he would know she was glad he got back safely.

"Oh, Raggedy!" Shaneeka's voice trembled.

They sat back down on the roof. They heard the boats all around them, and now they could see and hear something else, too – helicopters. They watched in amazement as the choppers hovered over the rooftops, lowering ropes and pulling people up into them.

"This is like some thing on TV," Poppa said.

"Except it isn't, it's really happening," Momma said. She sounded very sad and tired.

"Hmmph."

At last they heard a boat coming close to them again. The boat stopped next to their roof and the man in it said, "You folks like a lift?"

"Where to?" Poppa asked.

"We're just taking people to where it's dry, over near I-10 and the Superdome," he answered. He steered the boat right against the house, and held out his hand. Poppa picked Shaneeka up and lifted her to the man, who put her in the boat. Then Poppa helped Momma down off the roof, and then he stepped into the boat himself.

"We'll pick up as many people as we can, and then take you out of the flood," the man said. He had bottles of water in the boat and he gave them each one.

"But we have to stop and get Princess and Raggedy," Shaneeka told him.

"Who?" he asked.

"Princess and Raggedy, they're in the tree right there. Raggedy is my kitten."

"Oh, no, I'm sorry, but we can't take any pets," the man told her.

"What! Momma, if Raggedy can't go, I'm not going!" Shaneeka cried.

"Now, child, we have to do what we have to do," Momma said.

"But Momma, I can't leave Raggedy! I can't! He's just a baby; he won't know what to do without me!"

The man was starting the motor and turning the boat away from their house as Shaneeka said this. She realized that the boat really was going away from the tree the cats were in.

"No! No, we can't leave them – Poppa, make him stop! Momma, Momma!" Shaneeka was screaming. The boat rocked as she tried to stand up.

"Now, sit down!" the man said sternly.

"But I have to get Raggedy – I can't leave him! I'll never see him again. He might die!"

Momma reached for Shaneeka and held her

tightly. "Now, child, now, now," was all she could say, because she was crying just as hard as Shaneeka was.

Shaneeka twisted around in her mother's arms, and looked back towards the tree. She could just see the cats sitting in it, looking after the boat. She shrieked one last time, "Raggedy!" and buried her face in her mother's arms and sobbed, because her heart was breaking.

Poppa looked at the man driving the boat and shrugged.

"There's some folks that won't leave because we won't take their pets," the man said. "I hope they all make it."

"What's it like out there?" Poppa asked, waving his arm towards the rest of the city.

"Just like this, most places. Deeper in some, not as deep in others. The levees broke and the lake came into the city."

"Hmmph," said Poppa. "They been sayin' for years those levees need fixin' up. Now maybe they'll get to it. City won't never be the same, it seems like."

"Probably not. I know your daughter's broke

up about that kitten, but lots of folks lost more than that," the man said. "We've seen some awful things."

"I don't doubt you have," Poppa nodded. "We're just grateful you came along."

"I don't know that things are better where you're going, but at least it's dry land, such as it is." The man was quiet then.

Soon they came to another house with people on the roof. The man steered the boat near it and they got in. They did that once more, and the boat was full. Nobody said much. They just sat, stunned, families leaning against each other.

The man took them near a street high enough to be out of the water, and let them out. "You can stay here on the highway overpass, or you can walk over to the Superdome from here. I don't know as that's any better, there's an awful lot of people trying to crowd in there," he said.

"We thank you a lot," Momma said. "We'll do what we can now." Poppa got out of the boat, and Momma handed Shaneeka to him, because she was still crying, and did not even try to step out herself.

They all waded to the side of the road where it rose out of the water and stood on the sidewalk, looking around. Then one father said to his family, "Come on – we can get over to the building, at least we'll be under cover," and they started walking away.

Poppa looked towards the big building and shook his head. "I think we'll take our chances around here."

Another man, with a little boy just about Shaneeka's size said, "I believe we will, too." He turned away and leaned on the railing of the overpass.

The boy looked at Shaneeka and then at her Momma and Poppa. "Why are you crying?" he asked her, "Your family's all here, aren't they?"

Shaneeka sniffled. "Yes. Except that I had to leave Raggedy. He was my little kitten, and I'll never, ever see him again, I just know it."

The little boy shrugged and said, "I know. We had to leave my momma. She didn't get out of the house."

Shaneeka looked at the little boy and she knew then that as much as she would miss Raggedy, she was much, much luckier than many of the people who were caught in the terrible floods. "Oh," she whispered, and reached out and hugged him, and then both children were crying.

Shaneeka's Momma and Poppa went and stood next to the boy's father, and put their hands on his shoulders, and next thing, all three of them were crying, too.

CHAPTER 4

The two families spent that night and the next day on that roadway. They had some water that the man in the boat had given them, and on the second day some Army trucks came around with some food. Finally buses started appearing, and people got into them and were taken to other cities where they could have a place to stay.

Shaneeka and Momma and Poppa, and the boy and his father went to a small city in Texas. At first they went to a shelter with other hurricane victims. It was the farthest Shaneeka had ever been from home. She asked Momma and Poppa when they would be able to go back to their house. Momma said, "We'll see, child, we'll see," and Poppa just said "Hmmph."

Shaneeka knew by then that she might never see

Raggedy again and she hoped that he was all right. She would think about him often, and sometimes asked her parents if they thought he was safe. They did not always answer her, just patted her shoulder and hugged her. They knew she was sad, but they also knew that they were luckier than many people at that terrible time.

The family did not move back to New Orleans. After a while, Poppa got a job in their new city and they moved to an apartment. Momma did what she had done in New Orleans, cleaned people's houses.

One day Momma and Poppa met Shaneeka at her new school. They said they had a surprise and got onto a bus and rode to a street lined with small houses. They walked down the street, with Shaneeka asking at every corner, "Where are we going?" and her parents saying, "You'll see."

They stopped in front of a small house, opened the gate, and went up to the porch. Poppa took a key out of his pocket and opened the door!

Shaneeka gasped. "Is this our house?"

"Yes, it is," Momma answered. "Go look around."

Shaneeka did, running from the front room to

the kitchen to the bedrooms. One bedroom was large and one small, just like in their old house.

She went into the small room, and was surprised to see a cardboard box on the floor next to the bed. "Is this my room? What's in the box, is it something for me? Who put it here?" She asked questions so fast there was no time to answer in between them.

Momma laughed, "Yes, it is your room. I guess somebody put that box there and it seems to me the best way to find what's in it is to open it and look."

Shaneeka kneeled down by the box and tugged at the top of it. When the box moved, a loud "Mew!" came from it. Shaneeka looked at her parents hopefully. "Momma, Poppa, is it……" She pulled the top open and looked – and there sat a little black and white kitten!

"No, it's not Raggedy," her mother said. "He would be much bigger than that by now. But it's a kitten who needed a little girl, and we thought maybe a little girl needed a kitten."

Shaneeka reached in to the box. The kitten mewed again. She picked him up and looked at him. He did not look quite like Raggedy. This kitten had more white on his face, and less on his sides. Shaneeka looked at the kitten and the kitten looked at Shaneeka. He mewed and leaned forward and licked Shaneeka's nose. Then he started to purr.

"I think maybe the kitten thinks you could be his little girl," Momma said, smiling. "What do you think?"

Shaneeka looked at the kitten some more and then just hugged it tightly. She was sniffling a little bit and a tear slid down her nose. "His name can't be Raggedy," she said. "But I want to remember him, so this kitten's name will be Rags."

"That's a good name, and a good way to remember Raggedy," her mother said.

That night when they looked in on Shaneeka before they went to bed, Momma and Poppa saw the kitten snuggled next to their daughter's head on the pillow. Both of them had tears in their eyes. "I think we just might all be home again," Momma said, "but I surely would like to think that Raggedy and Princess are, too."

CHAPTER 5

When Shaneeka got into the boat, Raggedy was sure she would come and rescue him. After all, she always made sure he was near her. But when the boat sped away and left him and his mother in the tree, he mewed. He was scared and sad, because he thought Shaneeka had forgotten him. He even started to try to follow the boat, but Princess put a stern paw on his back and he stopped.

She settled back down on the tree limb and wrapped her tail around her paws, and Raggedy did the same thing. He was very hungry and thirsty, though, and he could not sit there for very long without mewing about that. Princess licked his head, but that did not make him stop wanting to have a drink of clean cool water. When night fell, the two cats curled up together on a branch safe above the water and went to sleep.

A cat perched high in a ruined house

They waited in the tree all the next day, but the family didn't return. Raggedy paced back and forth on their branch, sadly looking where the boat taking Shaneeka away from him had gone. The weather was hot, which made their thirst worse, and their bellies were very empty. Princess knew they had to do something. The water was going down a little bit, and she decided it was time to find some food. The closest place to look was in their house. She let Raggedy know he should follow her, and she started creeping down the trunk of the tree, holding on very tight with her sharp claws. Raggedy followed, staying very close to her. When they got to the water they both lapped some of it up. It tasted awful, though, so they did not take too much of it.

Still clinging to the tree, Princess looked towards the house. Then she leaped into the water and began swimming. Raggedy stayed on the tree. He had been in that water already, and he knew he didn't like it. He mewed to Princess, and mewed again, but she just kept swimming. He mewed one last time and then jumped into the dirty water, and began to swim as hard as he could. Princess slowed down and waited for him because she knew it was a long way for his little legs to paddle. It was a long way for her big legs to paddle!

When Raggedy caught up to her, she helped him again, and finally they got to the house. The water had gone down far enough that they could not reach the roof, so they paddled to the back door, which they had always used before. The water had forced the door open, and they swam inside. Momma's neat kitchen was now a big jumbled mess. The table and chairs, the coffeepot, dishtowels, and even the refrigerator were floating in the water!

The cats were so tired they just crawled onto the first thing they reached, which was the refrigerator, bobbing in the water. It was hard to hold on to because it was slanted and slippery.

All of the things inside the houses were left piled where they had floated in the water

They saw a cupboard door that had been pushed open by the water, and carefully walked up the side of the refrigerator until they could jump into it. This was more like it! It was fairly dry, and they could curl up without worrying about falling off.

Princess started to wash, because that is what cats do when they want to think about what to do next. Raggedy imitated her, but all he could think about was how hungry he was. He stood up on his wet and tired little legs, and started exploring the cupboard. He stepped around dishes and glasses, and found his way to the cupboard where Momma had stored food. Most of it was in cans, but he found a package of crackers and mewed loudly. He didn't know what was in the box, but he could tell by sniffing that it was something he could eat. Princess came to where he was, and together they scratched at the package until it tore into ribbons. They reached the crackers at last. Raggedy thought he had never eaten anything that good in his short life! They were dry, but he chewed and chewed until his little tummy was full. Then he was thirsty and tried to lap the water in the house again. It was so dirty he could not drink too much of it, which was a good thing because all the things in the water were not good for him.

The cats settled down in their cupboard and went to sleep. They were full and dry and that was all they wanted for now. They would wait for the water to go down and their people to come home. They could not know that Shaneeka and her family were on their way to someplace hundreds of miles away and would never come back.

After a few days the water went down even more, and they could see the counters. Raggedy jumped down and looked for more things to eat, but everything that had been on those counters had been swept away by the water. Finally they could see the floor of the kitchen. The crackers were gone and Raggedy was getting hungry again. He mewed and jumped to the floor and went to where the cats' dish had been. It was gone, of course. He went to Shaneeka's room. Her bed was soaked, and the dresser her clothes were in was tipped on its side. He looked under the bed and in the closet and behind the dresser but he did not find anything to eat. He jumped on the bed, thinking he could sleep there, but it was wet and smelly and not comfortable as it had been when Shaneeka was there and snuggled him under the covers with her. He mewed sadly and went back to the kitchen.

Princess had jumped to the floor, too, and looked for some food. She looked outside. There were still puddles of water everywhere, but there were some dry spots, like islands, between them. Princess meowed loudly for Raggedy, and he ran to her. The cats went outside into their yard. Everything was covered with a slimy layer of dark gooey sludge. It felt awful on their feet and was hard to walk in, but Princess knew they had to do it to try to find some food. It was over a week since the flood, and all they'd had to eat were those crackers.

She led Raggedy to the street. The mud and goo was there, too, and they had to keep weaving back and forth around puddles. Princess was looking for anything they could eat. She went to a neighbor's house, but when she looked inside, she knew there would not be anything left for them. That house was just as damaged by the water as their own.

After walking a long time, past many flood-ravaged houses and through what felt like miles of mud, they got to a little grocery store. The door and windows were broken, by the flood and by people who had been looking for food for themselves. The cats jumped in through a window and saw a jumble of tipped shelves and soaked packages of food lying everywhere.

*What the store might have looked like.
See the two chickens using this place for shelter?*

Princess stopped and sniffed, but Raggedy had already smelled something. He dashed across the muddy floor. A cooler for cold cuts and hot dogs had been knocked over. The meat, scattered all over the floor, had been water-soaked, but Raggedy did not care. He started gobbling it as fast as he could. Princess came over, and she started eating, too – not as fast as Raggedy, but she gnawed at the meat. When they had eaten as much as they could, they explored the store. One counter was still standing upright, and they jumped on it. First they washed, and then they went to sleep.

When they woke up, they went back to the case and ate some more of the meat. It was old and not very good because it had been in the water and then sitting out in very hot weather, but at least they had something to eat, and they were dry. They still had to drink the dirty floodwater, which tasted terrible, too. Raggedy was happy to be with his mother, but he missed Shaneeka. He missed playing with her, and being petted and snuggled

Since animals do not think ahead, Princess and Raggedy had no plans beyond being in the ruined store where there was food and water. On their third day in the store, they were awakened by dogs barking. They could hear that the dogs were very near the store.

Many, many animals had been left in the flooded parts of the city, because people were not allowed to rescue their pets. Now these animals ran loose, and they were all hungry. They were finding food and water wherever they could, and they were so hungry they would fight other animals for it.

Princess and Raggedy stood up on the counter just as three big dogs ran in to the store. They were barking because they smelled the meat the cats had been eating. Their noses led them straight to the case and each dog grabbed as much of the meat as it could and began to gobble it down. They growled and snapped at each other as they ate. They were just as hungry as the cats had been. These dogs were so busy eating, they didn't even know the cats were there.

Before Princess could stop him, Raggedy jumped down from the counter. That was his food! He had never met a dog, and did not know that they could hurt him. Princess knew, though. She had been chased by dogs before. Raggedy walked right up to the dogs and mewed to tell them that they were eating *his* meat. They turned to him and growled. One lunged at the kitten, ready to snap him in its powerful jaws. Princess jumped off the counter right on to its back with all her claws out! She yowled as loud as she could and the dog leaped back from Raggedy and swung his head, teeth flashing, trying to reach this thing that was clawing his back. The other dogs stopped eating and joined in.

A dog looking for food

Princess knew she could not fight three big dogs. She let go of the dog and jumped up onto the counter again. She meowed loudly to Raggedy, who had learned his lesson. He was right behind her. The two cats galloped across the counter and flung themselves through a broken window. They ran for their lives as the dogs, barking and howling, rushed out the door after them.

Princess was running as fast as she could, and so was Raggedy. They ran through puddles and across streets and over piles of trash that the floodwaters had left. The dogs were right behind them, baying so loudly that Raggedy thought his ears would burst. They ran and ran. Raggedy was getting tired, but the dogs were still behind them. Princess was looking for a place they could hide. She saw a fence ahead of her, with a tree and a house behind it. She turned her head and meowed loudly to Raggedy, and she jumped as hard and high as she could. She grabbed the wooden fence and pulled herself up, and then jumped from the fence to the tree and climbed it quickly. She turned to see where Raggedy was, but she didn't see him! She started back down the tree, and then she heard the dogs. Barking furiously, they ran right past the fence. Princess jumped back to the fence. She saw the dogs, sprinting down the street, and she could see something very small racing in front of them. It was Raggedy! He had not heard her meow or seen her jump onto the fence. Now he was by himself, running for his life.

Raggedy could not see Princess in front of him anymore, but he knew that the dogs were still behind him. He was getting very tired, but he kept running as fast as he could. There was a big building in front of him. Maybe Princess had run inside it. He scooted into the open door. He was in a huge warehouse full of coffee, coffee that no one would ever drink now. The flood waters had not spared this place either, and many of the sacks had fallen over and were still soaking wet.

Raggedy climbed up to the top of one of the big stacks and hid behind the bags. The dogs came charging through the door, barking loudly. Then they stopped. They sniffed around the piles of bags but they did not try to follow him. The strong smell of coffee masked Raggedy's scent, and as he peeked at the dogs milling around on the floor below, he knew he had escaped. The dogs barked once more. Then they turned and trotted out of the warehouse. They were satisfied that they had chased those pesky cats away from their food.

When the dogs were out of sight, Raggedy stood up on his hind legs and mewed as loudly as he could and swatted the air with his paws like a tiny lion, as if to say he would have swatted those dogs.

Coffee warehouse, where Raggedy might have hidden

He looked around and saw stacks and stacks of big bags that smelled like the coffee Momma made in the mornings, but he didn't see Princess. Raggedy did not know she was outside and far behind him. He mewed again, and again, but Princess did not answer him. He climbed over the towers of coffee bags, and went way into the big building looking for her. But he was very tired from running, and soon he crawled into a little space between two of the bags, and curled up and went to sleep.

Princess wanted to find Raggedy, but the dogs

were trotting back towards her. She hid, motionless and silent, until they went past where she was hiding. After they loped away, she headed down the street where Raggedy had run. She meowed and meowed at every place she thought he might have hidden. She slipped into the big warehouse, but she could not smell Raggedy because of the coffee, and he was so far inside and in between so many bags that he could not hear her. She climbed up on a pile of bags and meowed once more. Then she cautiously left the warehouse to look for her lost kitten. Late that afternoon, with blistered feet and aching legs, she was miles from where she last saw Raggedy. She searched for a safe place to rest.

Suddenly she saw people. They were walking towards her, and they were carrying boxes with wire-covered openings on the sides and handles on top in their hands. Maybe there was food in the boxes! She was nervous, but she stayed where she was, ready to run if they seemed threatening. They were talking quietly, and suddenly one person stopped and said "Look – there's a cat. Hey, kitty, pretty kitty, are you all alone? Come here, come on, that's a good kitty, don't run, we won't hurt you. Look, the poor thing's so thin, and shaking she's so scared. It's all right," the person repeated softly. "We won't hurt you. We want to help you."

As Princess listened, the person inched closer, and then held out a hand. "I bet you'd like some of this, wouldn't you?" a kind-sounding voice said. Princess sniffed. There was food in the hand reaching towards her! She meowed, and stretched her nose towards it and started eating the treats that were there.

As she did, another hand reached underneath her and picked her up. "There, now, we've got you. You're safe." Princess did not know the voice, but the hands were gentle. "Come along, now, we'll take you out of here," the rescuer said, and started to put her into one of the boxes they had been carrying. Suddenly Princess stiffened and meowed very loudly and sadly. Somehow she knew that if she got in to that box she would never see Raggedy, or Shaneeka or her family ever again.

"She's probably got someone she misses," the voice said. "You'll be all right—maybe they'll find you—and if not, you'll find a new family." They put

Princess into the carrier, and took her away with them. Princess was right, she never did see Raggedy again, but cats are different from people, and they do not remember their kittens or their humans the same way that people do. The rescuers were right, too, and she eventually did find a new family, and was a well-fed, happy cat again, warm and dry in a home a long way from New Orleans.

A rescued cat at Camp Katrina

CHAPTER 6

While this was happening to Princess, Raggedy was sleeping. He was just a few months old and he had done a lot of fast running that day. He woke up once and it was dark outside and he mewed a little bit and peeked out of his hiding place in the bags, and then he went back to sleep until daylight.

When he woke up, his tummy was rumbling and his mouth was dry and sore. He wondered where his mother was. If he could find her, she could help him find something to eat. She was always nearby. He stepped out of his little nest and mewed loudly. But Princess did not answer or come to him. He mewed again, even louder. But Princess still did not come. He had no way to know that she was many miles away, in a cage in a shelter run by the Humane Society of Louisiana. She was being fed and cared for.

He was all alone.

He mewed again, and jumped down from the big piles of bags of coffee to go look for her, and for something to eat. As he trotted through the warehouse, he saw something move ahead of him. He stopped short and stared, whiskers twitching. It was a mouse. Raggedy had never chased a mouse before, but Princess had told him about it, and he'd had lots of practice chasing things from playing with Shaneeka. He stayed very still, and then slowly, sliding on his belly, he crept towards the mouse. It was busy nibbling on the corner of a bag and didn't see him. He got closer and closer and then sprang at it. But he jumped from too far away and missed, and the mouse gave a startled squeak and dashed away. Raggedy chased it, but the mouse had been living in the warehouse for a long time. It knew where to run to get back to its hole. Raggedy watched the hole for a while, but the mouse did not come out again.

He looked around the big building for Princess, but of course she wasn't there. He didn't find anything to eat, either, and after a while he wandered outside. He sat down and gazed up and down the street in front of the warehouse. He didn't know what to do. He didn't know which way to go. He mewed, but nobody answered him. One direction looked as bleak as another, with big oily pools of water, torn and empty houses, cars and furniture and trees lying where the floods had swept them. And, Raggedy realized, there were no people anywhere. Finally he started down the street, hoping he could find something to eat and some good water.

Raggedy did not know it, but he was just one of thousands of animals who were all alone in the houses and streets of the city. The people who had been stranded in the floods could not bring their pets when they were rescued. Some, like Princess and Raggedy, were living on the streets.

Others were still inside houses. They had been left behind when their owners evacuated, with a little food and water because the people thought they would be back in just a few days. No one knew that it would be weeks and weeks before anyone could come back to rescue their pets, if they could come back at all. Some brave people found ways to get to their homes, even though it was dangerous, and rescued their animal friends. Others were not so lucky.

People from every state in the country, and even other countries, like Canada, came to New Orleans to try to save the animals, spending long hours catching as many as they could.

Rescuers: Phil, LuAnn and Cassandra, getting ready to look for animals

They came day after day and took hundreds of abandoned pets to shelters outside of the destroyed city. From there, the animals went to other shelters and then to foster and forever homes all over the country. Everyone hoped that the owners would someday find their pets, and they tried as many ways as possible to make this happen.

But Raggedy did not know any of this. He only knew that he was lonesome, and he was hungry and thirsty. He went in to houses looking for food, but he did not find anything. He looked in the piles of trash that were lying on the streets, but there had been many animals on these same streets, and they had already found just about everything there was to eat. Once Raggedy jumped to a windowsill to look inside a store, but there were hungry dogs inside, so he quickly and quietly jumped down and ran away. In one house he found some wet, moldy bread. It tasted awful, but he ate it anyway. He curled up on a counter and slept inside that house.

The world seemed to have been turned upside down. There were puddles and trash everywhere, cars on top of fences, and houses collapsed by the force of the wind and the water. Boats sat in the middle of the streets.

Raggedy saw many strange sights like this

The water was still deep in some places and he had to go around it. Mud covered everything, and Raggedy's feet were always wet and dirty. Some nights he was able to get into a house to sleep, but other times he slept outside, hiding as best he could under piles of trash. He did not know where he was going. He just wandered the city, hoping that he would find Princess, or Shaneeka and her family, and that they would take him home and feed him and cuddle him. Besides being hungry, Raggedy missed people. He was a people cat. He liked being petted and played with and fussed over.

One day he came to a street that was not wet and muddy. He saw people! He was so happy. Now he might get something to eat, and someone might pet him. He peeked into the first open door he saw. There was a big room, with many small tables, and a long bar on one side of it. A few people were sitting at the tables, and others were sitting on stools at the bar. Raggedy did not know what sort of place this was, but it had people in it. He slowly walked through the door and toward the bar, where he could see people reaching into small bowls and putting little things into their mouths, sort of like the cat food Shaneeka used to give him. His little nose twitched and the tip of his little tail twitched, too. He couldn't stand it anymore, he was so hungry! He jumped onto an empty stool and quicker than quick he jumped onto the bar. He padded over to a bowl and sniffed. It didn't smell quite like the cat food he was used to, but he started eating anyway. It didn't taste like cat food, either, but it did taste good!

"Hey, there's a cat eating the peanuts!" someone said.

"Maybe he'd like a beer," one of the people laughed. Raggedy just kept eating. He ate every peanut in that bowl and started towards the next one.

"Oh, no you don't," the man sitting by the dish said, and he grabbed Raggedy. "We don't have any food as it is, and I'm not sharing with a scrawny kitten!" And he went to the door and threw Raggedy back onto the street.

Raggedy got up and shook his head. He wasn't hurt, but he was surprised. He had never had people do anything but pet him and feed him and be nice to him. He took a few steps back towards the bar, but the man stood in the doorway, and as Raggedy got close he kicked at him. "I said no!" the man shouted. Raggedy dodged the foot, and backed away a little bit. The man started to walk towards him and Raggedy turned around and fled.

By this time a woman had come to the doorway. "Now what did you go and do that for?" she asked. "He was cute and he wouldn't have eaten much. We survivors have to stick together."

"Yeah, well, I'll stick together with my own, without animals taking what little I have to eat," the man said, and stomped back inside.

The woman walked down the street a ways calling, "Here, Kitty, Kitty, Kitty. Come on back, little cat." But Raggedy was gone.

Raggedy was running again, but he was too tired to run far. He was getting weaker because he had not eaten for so long. He ducked into a small alley that had many cans and boxes and bags of trash in it. There was still no electricity, and the restaurants and bars were throwing away all the spoiled food that had been in their coolers. Raggedy could smell food, but it smelled very bad. It had been out in the hot weather for so long.

Farther down the alley, he spotted some bags that had been torn open. He was just about to look inside to see what he could eat when he heard growling. There were dogs in the alley looking for food, too! One growled again, and another barked, and Raggedy fled as fast as he could, out of the alley and down the street. He was not taking any chances with dogs, no matter how much he wanted food!

Now he was not sure that being near people was such a good idea. As much as he liked them, he had discovered that not all people like little cats. There also seemed to be more dogs here, nearer the people and the garbage. Maybe he was better off back where he'd come from. The only trouble was that he did not know where that was, or how he could get there. Raggedy stopped running and looked around, but everything looked the same. He sighed sadly and started walking again.

Raggedy walked and walked. Sometimes he started down a street only to have to turn back because there was still water there.

He walked through streets that looked like this

By the time it was getting dark he had gone many blocks. He was a long way from the bar where the man had thrown him outside, but he was a long way from his home, too. He crawled underneath the steps of a large building and went to sleep, hungry, thirsty, and lonely.

In the morning he started walking again, looking for food, water, and a safe place to stay. He saw many frightening things, and everywhere he went there was destruction from the hurricane and the floods. In one place, he saw a glow in the sky and flames shooting into the air. Fires were starting in some parts of the city, and the firemen were doing what they could to put them out. He could hear sirens and shouting, and smell smoke, so he knew it would not be a good idea to go in that direction.

Once he saw some people again, but when he got close, they shouted at him and one man ran towards him, and threw stones. Raggedy was frightened and turned and ran away as fast as he could.

It took him several days of walking on his small, sore, and tired legs and feet to get away from the larger buildings and back to where there were mostly small houses. He had walked many miles but he somehow felt safer.

Raggedy spent many days just wandering from house to house looking for food and safe places to sleep. Many nights he climbed into the kitchen cupboards of a house, because somehow those felt cozy, and because they were often the driest places he could find. Now and then he saw dogs, and he always ran from them. He did not know if they would chase him or not, and he did not want to find out. He saw other cats, but they did not want to have a stranger join them. They were just as hungry as he was.

Even worse than not having food was not having water to drink. He kept trying to drink the water in the puddles that were still all over, but it was filthy. He somehow knew that if he drank much he would be very sick.

One afternoon he heard thunder rumbling. The sky got dark and it started to rain very hard. Raggedy ran to the nearest building. It was a small store with a broken door.

This might have been the store he went into

There was a grate across the opening, but Raggedy was so skinny he could fit through the bars. He found a few little packages on a counter that smelled like what had been in the dish at the bar. He tore one open with his teeth, and gobbled the peanuts down even faster than he had eaten the other ones. He stayed inside the store until the rain stopped. When it did, he went outside and found something wonderful—a big pan with fresh rainwater in it! He stayed in the store until the peanuts and the water were gone. Then he went back out onto the streets.

Raggedy's life had become a search for food and

water, and for safe places to sleep. Many of the houses had fences around them, and he was so weak from being hungry that it was getting harder and harder for him to jump or climb over them. He was sleeping in piles of trash again. Many of the places he walked now were covered with dark gray chunks of dried sludge, two or three inches thick. This was the mud and dirt and oil that had been in the flood water, the goo that he and Princess had walked through when they first left their house.

On many of the houses were big spray-painted messages like "No Animals," "4 dogs, SPCA called," or "Empty." The police and National Guard had been searching for survivors of the storm. When they found anything they would write it on the house so that rescuers would know where to stop. Sometimes the writing was sad, like "Dead dog under house." Too many animals had drowned in their homes, or had not been able to live without food.

By now people were coming back to some of the houses. They were pulling things from their ruined homes and piling them by the streets. Raggedy tried going up to the people, to see if they would pet him and feed him, but they were busy and did not notice a little kitten. He looked through the piles of rubble, but there was nothing for him to eat.

He found one place where people had piled up all sorts of things they had found in the streets—lawn furniture, pots and pans, pieces of siding from houses, an old tool box, even a pet carrier and a shopping cart! Someone had put a sign on it that read "TOXIC ART – This Exhibition Will Kill You!"

The pet carrier in the pile of trash

He could not read the words, but he climbed around in the pile sniffing at everything. The pet carrier still smelled a little bit like cat, so he crawled into it and took a nap, just because it had been so long since he was even close to another animal. When he woke up he started walking again.

He walked past a schoolyard that had the dried sludge all over it. He walked past boats in people's yards, and a house with one side sitting on a car. He saw a church that had collapsed—but the steeple on top of it was still upright. One house was completely demolished, but a bicycle still leaned against the concrete front steps. Another had a glass case with many pretty dolls in it – they were dirty from the flood water, but they were still pretty, and he looked at them a long time, remembering the doll that Shaneeka had and how she had played with it and him together.

The water had been over the top of the head of the doll on top of the case

It was almost a month since the hurricane and the floods that had taken Raggedy's home and people and mother away from him. He had been on his own for almost a quarter of his entire short life. He had almost drowned, almost been caught by dogs, and now was almost starved. He found fewer and fewer morsels of food. His ribs and backbone stuck out. He also was sick from something called ringworm, which was making the fur on his head and neck fall out. He was too tired to wander anymore and was living in an empty house now, sleeping more and more as he grew weaker. His only hope for food now was catching bugs or an occasional mouse. He was glad Princess had taught him how to hunt. But even that was hard for him now.

Just when he thought things could not get worse, it started to rain very hard. The winds blew almost as noisily as they had before, when his house got flooded. Raggedy ran into a house and huddled under a pile of furniture and hoped the water did not come into the house as it did the last time. He did not know if he could stand it, and was sure he did not have the strength to survive another flood. Fortunately, Hurricane Rita did not do as much damage in New Orleans as Katrina had done.

After the storm, he ventured out of the house. Even though he had less and less energy, he knew he had to keep looking for food and water. The storm had left new rain water, and that helped him, but he was so hungry, and getting weaker every day. He would have cried, because he was so lonely, so hungry and thirsty, and so discouraged. But cats cannot cry, and they have a strong, inborn survival instinct, which took over whenever Raggedy wanted to give up. He didn't know that in many parts of the ruined city people were putting out food for the animals, and pans of fresh water for them to drink.

Cats eating food left for them by rescuers

He did not know that everywhere, rescuers were looking for animals to save, but it was a slow process. They looked into all the houses and down all the streets of all the parishes of the city, but it was a big place. If Raggedy had known any of this, he would have gone to find the food, or to find someone to rescue him. Once, he thought he heard people's voices, but by the time he woke up and looked outside, he did not see anyone. He thought maybe he had dreamed it, and he mewed and went back to sleep, because it was nice to dream that he had people around again, and enough to eat and drink without having to hunt for it.

CHAPTER 7

Four weeks had passed since the storm, and Raggedy had been all alone for most of that time. His wandering had brought him back to Desire Street again, not too far from his home with Princess and Shaneeka and her family. It was autumn now, and the nights were cooler. Keeping warm was taking a toll on his starving little body, too.

Even though there were no people living around where he was, he could sometimes hear cars. He remembered from seeing cars drive past the house he lived in with Shaneeka that cars meant people, and people meant food and petting.

It was thirty two days after the hurricane. Raggedy heard a car, closer than the others had been. He meowed. He sat on the sidewalk and meowed as loudly as he could. He meowed and meowed as if he knew that his life depended on it.

He could hear the car coming closer and looked towards the noise. Then, he saw a van with two women inside it coming down the street. He stood up and meowed some more and the van stopped beside him. The door opened and before the driver could get out, he had jumped right into the van. He was so glad to see people!

"Well," the woman sitting next to the driver said, "I guess you did want to get rescued." Raggedy meowed again. He had a lot to tell these people.

"Look how skinny. Poor little kitten—it must be so hungry," the driver said. "Welcome aboard, little cat. Guess what? You're safe now." She picked Raggedy up and held him as they got out of the van and looked to see if there were any more animals nearby to rescue.

Rita holding Streetcar when she and Cassandra rescued him

Raggedy started to purr. He believed her. "Listen to that!" the other woman said. "Saying thank you. Bet it would say thank you to some food, too."

Food! That, thought Raggedy, was the finest thing he had ever heard!

The van was filled with animal carriers and food and bottles of water and leashes, for the animals they hoped they would find to rescue. They put him into a small carrier and gave him some of the food and water. Raggedy ate and drank until his little tummy was round. Then he started to meow some more. He meowed the whole day, as the two women drove around looking for animals that were still alone on the streets. His meowing made any dogs who heard it bark, and then the women would stop the van and try to catch them. By the end of the day, there were a lot of dogs in the van with Raggedy.

Raggedy was a little nervous about being in a van with the dogs, and he hissed the first time the women put one inside. "Don't worry, little kitten, they can't get at you", one of them said. He ate and drink a little bit each time the van stopped, and watched as the people put more dogs, in carriers, into the van. They were right, none of the dogs could get at him. Most of them did not pay any attention to the little kitten; they were too busy having some food and water themselves. They had been out on the streets since the hurricane and floods, too.

By the end of the day, there were a lot of animals in the van with Raggedy. When it got dark, the rescuers came back to the van and it moved for a long time. It finally stopped in a place that smelled very different from the city. That smelled like mud and decay. This just smelled like clean air. The women got out and the one wearing the hat took Raggedy's carrier. He looked around as much as he could, but he could only see one small house, and lots of trees.

Raggedy had been brought to a shelter owned by the Humane Society of Louisiana. It was in the country, near a place named Tylertown, Mississippi. There were people there from all over the United States and Canada, caring for the rescued animals.

The woman carried Raggedy to a table with people sitting and standing around it. "We've got six dogs and this one kitten," she said.

Nobody said anything. Then a woman standing behind the table said, "Here, give it to me—nobody's in 'Cat Land,' I guess. I like cats; I'll take care of it."

If Raggedy had been able to read, he would have seen the tag on the person's shirt that said her name was Barbara. He just looked out of the front of the carrier as she took him inside, and set him on the floor. He could see cages that had other cats inside. Some of them meowed, and he mewed back.

"Yes, get acquainted," Barbara said. "You'll be together for a while." She put a towel and a tray with litter in it, and dishes with food and water in a cage, and then bent down and opened the carrier and reached for Raggedy. He did not need a second invitation! He scrambled onto her chest, and wrapped his little front legs as far as they could go around her neck, put his nose up against her chin, and started to purr.

"Well, look at you. You're glad to be rescued, huh?" she said. "I guess a little petting would be a good thing," and she stroked Raggedy's bony back. "Oh, dear, you've got some ringworm going on there," she said when she looked at his head and neck. "Well, that's curable, once you get to a home."

Raggedy just purred more, and rubbed his nose against her chin.

"Yes, I know, but much as I would like to stand here and pet a kitten, there is more work to do," she said, as she detached Raggedy's claws from her shirt. "So, it's into the cage for you, little…" She turned him upside down and looked at his back side "….little boy," she said, as she put him in the cage.

He mewed and pressed his nose against the bars.

"I know, I know," she said. "I'll be back soon."

CHAPTER 8

Raggedy had arrived at Camp Katrina. It was the same shelter where Princess had been, although she was not there anymore. She was taken on a big, fancy bus by people who had come from Long Island, in New York. They took Princess because she was so pretty, and they thought they could find someone who would like to care for her until her family found her, or if they did not, someone who could give her in a nice, loving home forever.

The carriers on the seats inside the fancy bus

The people at the shelter knew that all these animals had people somewhere, who missed them as much as Shaneeka missed Raggedy. They filled out a paper with information for each one, so that maybe someday they could be reunited with their owners. When that happened it made everyone feel so good! Every day, people were coming to the shelter, ninety miles from New Orleans, hoping that their pets would be there. If they were not, they were told to not give up hope, try the other shelters. Many of the owners were far away, like Shaneeka and her family, and would not be able to come get them. The people at the shelter vowed to make sure each of those animals had a chance to have a good home.

Back outside, everyone was busy with the dogs that had been in the van with Raggedy, and with dogs that came in another van. More dogs were rescued than cats. First, each dog got a bath and had its picture taken.

Laurie and Phil washing a dog

Then it was put into a cage with food and water for the night. The next day each one was checked by the veterinarian and given shots. After that, they could go into a bigger run with other dogs. The cats were not given baths, because people knew how cats feel about that, but they did get papers filled out with information about where they were found and what they looked like, just like the dogs. The veterinarians checked the cats, too, and gave them shots to keep them from getting sick.

Barbara went to the table and asked, "Is there any paperwork for that kitten that just came in?" Someone pointed to a note on a piece of paper: B&W kitn

– stray, found 2400 block Desire. Walking back inside, she mused, "Found on Desire Street, huh? Hey, little guy," she said to Raggedy, "Your name is gonna be Streetcar. You're named after a great play."

"My name is Raggedy," he mewed, but of course she could not understand kitten-talk. She filled out a form and put it on the door of his cage. Raggedy was trying to use his litter pan but he had been hungry and thirsty for so long he had nothing to do in it. A veterinarian noticed that.

"He needs to be hydrated. Let's give him some sub-cu," which is veterinarian shorthand for giving an animal fluids through a needle under its skin. Barbara held Raggedy while a needle was put into his back, and the life-giving fluids dripped into his emaciated body. "He's skinny and needs that ringworm treated," the vet said, "But his eyes look good, and he's active enough. He should be fine."

Raggedy did not like the needle, but he did feel better after they were done. He could see many more cats in cages all around him. He thought he could talk to them tomorrow, because he was very tired right now. The food and water and fluids had made him feel much better.

"I'm going to cover you up so you can sleep," Barbara said, "and some one will be here to take care of you in the morning."

Raggedy curled up and mewed contentedly. He was asleep before she finished wrapping towels around his cage.

In the morning, someone took the towels off and said, "Oh, look at the cute new kitten!" He got more food and water, and someone gave him a pill, and then put some oily medicine on his head and neck where the fur was gone. "This is for your ringworm," he was told.

His cage was on the corner of a hallway, and many people walked past it during the day. Almost everyone stopped to say hello and pet him, and if they didn't, he soon learned that if he stuck a paw out of the cage and mewed, they would. He liked all the attention! He was so happy to be where there were people to take care of him again.

Raggedy/Streetcar reaching for someone to pet him

He talked with the other cats, and each one had a story almost like his. Some had been trapped inside houses. Their owners had left food and water, but that was gone many days before the cats were rescued. Many had been on the streets like Raggedy. A few had been brought to other shelters by people whose homes had been destroyed by the floods and who had to move away from the city they had lived in all their lives. Raggedy listened to the stories and thought he was lucky that the rescuers had found him. The other cats all thought they were lucky, too.

The woman named Barbara would come to see Raggedy two or three times every day. She always called him Streetcar, and he always told her his name was Raggedy. One day she said, "How would you like to come live in New York, Streetcar? I said I wouldn't bring any animals back with me, but I think I'm going to have to." She put a piece of paper on his cage that said he would be her cat.

A few days after that she said to him, "We're going home today, Streetcar. It's a long ride in a car, but you'll like what's at the end of it."

Raggedy didn't understand, but by now he had decided that even if she didn't know his name, he liked Barbara. He wouldn't mind living with her. Later that day she took him out of his cage. The veterinarian gave her some pills and medicine, and she signed some papers, and then she put him into a carrier with a fresh towel, a little pan with clean litter at one end, and little dishes of food and water at the other. "Let's head north, Streetcar," she said. She fastened the seat belt around his carrier. "Don't want you to fall off, do we?"

The next thing Raggedy knew the car was moving. He mewed a few times, and she put a finger through the front of the carrier to pet him. "It's a long ride, but you've got the easy part." Raggedy agreed.

They rode for a long time. When it was dark, Barbara said, "Time to find a home for the night, Streetcar." She took his carrier and a bag of food up some stairs and into a room that had two beds in it. "Now, little guy, I just bet you'd like to get out and move around, after being in cages and carriers for so long," she said, and opened the door of the carrier.

This was the first time Raggedy had been able to run around in almost a week. He stepped out of the carrier and took a few cautious steps, and then he raced all around that room! But he always made sure he knew where the person was. When she went into a small room next to the room with the beds, he went right along. Then she went into a smaller room with a door he could almost see through, and he heard water running. He wasn't sure about that, but no water came out where he was. He sat down and waited, and soon she stepped out of the strange small room. She was all wet! He mewed, because the last people he had seen who were wet were in the flood. She reached down to pet him. "I know, you're afraid of another flood. Don't worry, little guy," she said. "That sure felt good, Streetcar. After that many days in the hot sun without a shower handy—well, you wouldn't know, but it feels good to people!" Raggedy wondered if it felt as good as when Princess used to wash him, or even when he washed himself.

Raggedy had to go back in his carrier to sleep, but he was able to run around the room for a few minutes the next day before they got back into the car. They rode a very long way that day, and when they stopped that night it was colder outside, and raining. He was able to run around the motel room again, and even though he ate a big meal, he tried to grab bits of Barbara's supper. She laughed when he peeked over the edge of the table, with just his little face showing and gave him some people-food for treats. When she put him back in the carrier and turned out the lights to go to sleep he mewed and mewed until she brought him next to her bed. "I can't let you out, but I'll be right here, little guy," she said. He thought that was all right and went to sleep, too.

CHAPTER 9

The next day they rode a long way again. It was dark when the car stopped and Barbara said, "We're home, Streetcar. You hang out here and I'll go fix up your room. I can't let you out in the house with the other cats, not while you still have the ringworm."

Room? Other cats? Raggedy didn't know exactly what all that meant, but when he was carried into the house he could smell other cats. When the carrier was set down, two cat faces came and peered inside. One was very round, and had big eyes, and was partly white and partly brown-striped. The other was two-tone brown, and had blue eyes and dark brown ears. Raggedy went to the door and sniffed. "Who are you?" the two-tone brown cat asked.

"I'm Raggedy," he said. "But the person calls me Streetcar."

"Huh," the cat with the big eyes replied. "You're just a kitten."

The brown cat muttered, "Hmmph. I don't know that we needed a kitten." She reminded Raggedy of Shaneeka's father.

"We'll have to think about this," the other cat said.

They started to turn away, and Raggedy called, "Wait! Who are you?"

The big-eyed cat said, "I'm Beauty Queen."

Raggedy knew his cat manners and he said, "And you are very beautiful." Beauty Queen just nodded to him.

"I'm Mocha," the two-toned cat said. "I'm a Siamese. I've been here the longest."

"It's very nice to meet you. You must be very wise," Raggedy said.

Barbara watched this, but of course she did not know what they were saying. "Now that you've met, it's time to put you in quarantine, Streetcar," she said. She put the carrier in a room by itself, and took Raggedy out. "You've got your own litter box and water dish," she told him. "You'll go to the vet on Tuesday, and after that we'll see how the ringworm clears up. When it does, you can come out into the house with the girls."

She sat with Raggedy for a few minutes and petted him, and then went out and closed the door. Raggedy mewed. He wanted to be with his new person! But then he looked around the room and saw that he had a lot of space to run and play. Barbara came back later and gave him some food. She turned the light out. "Bedtime," she said. "I'll see you in the morning."

In the morning she came in and fed him, gave him his medicine, and cleaned his litter pan. He didn't see that this was very different from the shelter, except that he had more space to move around in. "I thought she said it was going to be different when we got home," he thought, but he was willing to wait and see what happened. No matter what, this was better than being all alone in the city, not having food or water, and not having a person at all.

Streetcar, on his first day in his new home

A few days later, Barbara put him in the carrier again. "It's a much shorter ride this time, Streetcar, we're just going to the veterinarian," she told him. It was. When she lifted him out of the carrier, she put him on a small, high table. Two women looked at him all over, felt his sides and legs and stomach and back, stuck needles into him and fussed over him. "He's healthy except for the ringworm, and needing food," they said.

He could have told them he needed food! What did they think when he hadn't had any all that time?

But he was polite and didn't say anything.

"These pills will cure the ringworm. Keep him away from the other cats until they are gone. He's a cutie!"

Raggedy mewed, "Thank you." He spent several more days in the room by himself, and was given a pill every morning. Then one day Barbara opened the door and said "Come on out." He slowly walked out of the room and looked around. Wow! There were five other rooms, with lots of space for a kitten to run around in. There was even a tree that he thought he could climb, but it fell over when he tried, because it was not strong enough to hold him. He galloped all through the house. He found the dish with food for the other cats in it and tried some. It was good! He found the big litter box and used it, and felt quite grown up.

Then he found Mocha and Beauty Queen. Neither of them wanted to play kitten games or run or tussle the way he and the rest of Princess's kittens had. They were older cats and just wanted to sleep in the sun.

He kept trying, but they kept saying no. He had almost as much fun playing by himself. He found rubber bands in Barbara's desk and threw some of those to the floor to chase. He found toys that Mocha and Beauty Queen had played with when they were younger. And, when he was tired of playing, he could curl up and take a nap in the sun that came through a big window into the living room, on one of the cat beds that were on the floor.

For a while, he spent nights in the room by himself, but one day two other people came to the house. One was another woman, Sara, and the other was a tall boy named Stephen, whose skin was almost the same color that Shaneeka's had been. Women had always been nice to him, but Raggedy remembered that there had been men who had chased him, and that a man had thrown him out of the place that had the peanuts. So when the boy tried to pet him, he ran away. The boy knew what to do, though. He took some cat treats and held them in his hand, down near the floor. Raggedy could not resist any food, and he slowly walked up to Stephen's hand, sniffed, and started chewing the treats. While he ate, Stephen petted his head. Raggedy knew then that this boy would not hurt him, and he purred. That night he was allowed to stay outside the room, because Stephen was sleeping there. Since he was a well-behaved cat, he was able to keep on doing it.

Raggedy was a happy kitten. He got treats every morning and after supper, he had plenty of food and water, he had soft places to sleep and toys to play with. His very favorite treats were peanuts, and every time he heard the jar rattle he would come racing from wherever he was to get some. One day he discovered something people called peanut butter. It was soft and gooey. He just loved that, even though it stuck to the inside of his mouth and he had to twist his tongue to lick it off!

He was growing and gaining weight and his ribs and backbone did not stick out anymore. He was getting to be quite a handsome cat, in fact. He would always remember being hungry, and whenever someone was fixing or eating food he would get as close as he could to see if they would give him any of it, just in case he got stranded without food again. Once he sat down right in a frying pan that was on the counter to watch, and could not understand why the person laughed at him.

The cat dishes were always full of food and water, but Raggedy remembered being thirsty, too, and he needed to be sure that he could get a drink any time he wanted one. He would jump into the sink and lap water out of the dishes soaking there, and whenever the spigot ran he would lean in close and try to lap it up, and put his paws into it. If the water was being used to wash dishes or hands, he would play with the soapsuds in the sink. He would also come into the bathroom and climb gingerly onto the side of the bathtub—he had seen water in there and wanted to make sure it was going down through the little holes in the bottom, and not rising and rising as he had once seen water do. Sometimes he would sit on the edge of the tub when Barbara stood under the water coming out of the pipe above her head, to make sure that she did not get caught by the water.

There was a stand by a window that he could sit on and look outside, and he could see squirrels and birds in the yard. He muttered to himself about what he would do to them if he was out there, but they could not hear him. There was a big bushy plant on a shelf, and sometimes he would climb into it to see if there was anything to eat or play with in there. He thought that this was a good place to be living, and slowly he started to forget some of the bad things that had happened to him when he was a lost kitten on Desire Street.

One day Mocha and Beauty Queen asked Raggedy about what his life was like before he came to live with them, and he told them about Shaneeka and the storms and floods and being alone. Both of the older cats were quiet for a long time when he was finished. Then they looked at each other, and Mocha said to him, "Well, I'm still not sure we really needed a kitten, but you needed a home, and this will be a good one. I myself came from the shelter many years ago, and I've been happy here."

Beauty nodded and said "I had another person, but she was moving and couldn't take me. She cried when she brought me here. I miss her, but this is a good place for a cat." Then they both said, "Welcome to our home," and Raggedy licked their heads and said, "Thank you."

Sometimes when the front door opened he would look outside, and think how strange it looked. He could not see any houses, but he could see many trees, and grass that looked brown and dry. He asked Mocha and Beauty Queen what was out there and they told him, "Trees and grass and flowers in the summer. But now it is too cold to go outside. We'd rather stay in and sleep in the sun." Raggedy did not understand what they meant by cold. One day when Barbara was bringing bags of people-food through the door, he sneaked out. The air smelled very different than it did in New Orleans—this was clean and dry air. It was very cold, too. Mocha and Beauty Queen had been right. He crept out onto the deck that went around the front of the house, but he did not get a chance to see much.

"Oh, no you don't," scolded Barbara. She gathered him into her warm arms. "You don't go outside by yourself, Little Mister."

One morning he looked outside and the ground was all white! He ran to Mocha and Beauty Queen, because by now he had found out that they knew many important things to teach him. "What's wrong with the ground?" he asked. "It's all white!"

"That's just snow," Beauty said.

"What's snow?" he asked.

"Snow is cold and wet," Mocha answered, "and it's not fun to play or even walk in!"

But Raggedy wanted to find out for himself. When Barbara opened the door, he sneaked outside again. He took a couple of steps onto the deck and suddenly his paws were colder than they had ever been before and as wet as they had been in the flood! He jumped up onto a shovel that was leaning against the house and mewed very loudly.

Barbara came to get him. "A little cold on the paws, is it?" she asked him. She carried him back inside and wiped his paws off and rubbed them a little to warm them up. Raggedy mewed and purred. He was satisfied that he did not want to go play in the snow!

Raggedy had toy mice, and little balls to play with. He would bat at the toys with his paws and chase them around the floor, and then catch them and hold them in his front paws and roll onto his back and bite them and dig at them with his back claws. Sometimes he would just run through the house, and jump onto some of the shelves and counters and chests that were in different rooms.

He liked to run to the bathroom doorway, and then see how high he could jump up onto the sides of the door. He would wrap his legs around the door frame and put his claws into the wall, and hang there. As he got bigger and stronger, he could jump almost to the top of the door! Barbara laughed at him, but when she saw his claw marks in the wall she sighed. "I guess I can fix those when you grow up and don't do it any more," she said. "I think you might be practicing to get away from another flood. Don't worry, there won't be one of those here." Raggedy wondered how she knew that was exactly what he was doing—making sure that if he had to, he could jump high into a tree to escape the dirty, rushing water that had changed his life forever.

He learned that there were some things he should not do. He would be called "Bad cat!" and put into his carrier for a timeout when he did them. A few times, he was put in it for trying to play too roughly with Beauty or Mocha. They would yowl and Barbara would come and grab him and tell him 'NO!" in a very stern voice.

A few months after he came to the house, he saw Barbara putting brightly colored dangling things on the small pine tree that was in the living room. He thought those were new toys for him. When she had many of them on all the limbs of the tree, she went to fix a cup of tea. Raggedy went to the tree and started to swat at the ones on the lower branches. Then he saw the ones higher up, and jumped to swat at those. When he came down from that jump, he hit one of the lower branches and an ornament went flying off of it and hit the chest next to the tree. It broke with a crash! Barbara came running and her voice was very angry! He ran and hid under the bed where she could not reach him and stayed there for a long time.

He also learned that there were holes in the floor where warm air came out. Mocha had taught him that, and when it was cold each of them would lie on one of those holes until Barbara picked them up and moved them, saying, "If you don't cover the heat vents, we all can be warm, not just you cats!"

Raggedy was happy. He was thinking less and less about his life on Desire Street, and his mother and his people there. He was learning things from Mocha and Beauty Queen, and he played and ran every day. He was almost all grown up, but he would never be a very big cat, because of the growing he did not get to do when he had no food after the flood.

But, as good as his new life was, there was some sadness, too. Mocha had not been feeling well for a long time, even before Raggedy came to live with them. Now she was spending most of her time sleeping. She still liked her special cat food and treats, but she ate hardly anything. It was hard for her to move around. One morning when Raggedy went to check on everyone in the house, he found Mocha lying in the room he had been in when he first got there. She could not move. Barbara called the veterinarian. She brought Mocha out into the front room, and put her into one of the cat beds and covered her up. Beauty Queen and Raggedy sat nearby. Mocha tried to get up. Twice, she meowed sadly, and then closed her eyes.

"Oh, Mocha," Barbara said, and was very quiet for a long time.

Raggedy went to sniff Mocha, and Beauty Queen told him that she would not know he did it. "She has crossed the Rainbow Bridge," Beauty told him.

"What's that?" he asked.

"It's where we all go one day, to wait for our people," she told him. "Mocha is there, and when we go there we will see her again."

Raggedy thought about this and then he asked, 'When will I go there?"

"Not for a long time. You are just a young cat. I am older, but I won't go for a while."

"Good," Raggedy said. He still remembered the terrible time after the flood. "I don't want to be alone." Then he asked, "Will I see my old family there, and my mother?"

"You might," said Beauty Queen. "And I don't think you will ever be alone here. I think that there will always be company for you."

While they were talking, Barbara had gone outside. When she came back in she picked up Mocha, whom she had wrapped in a nice warm cloth, and gently carried her out. When she came back in the house, her arms were empty, and her face was wet with tears. She sat down and hugged Raggedy and Beauty for a long time. They licked her cheeks, and then sat quietly and purred.

CHAPTER 10

Barbara bought Raggedy a handsome harness to wear. When the weather got warmer, one day she attached a leash to it. "Come on, Streetcar, it's time to start learning where your territory is." She took him outside and walked around the house with him. Part of the way he walked on the leash and part of the way she carried him. He looked at everything, amazed. He loved the way the grass tickled his paws. He stared up into the trees he'd seen through the windows. Birds hopped and sang in the branches, and squirrels chased each other. He decided that he had to get out by himself and do some real exploring.

A few days later, Barbara opened the door and before she could stop him, he ran out, dove through a hole in the deck and disappeared underneath the house! It was dark and there were lots of things to smell, including some strange animal he had never smelled before. It was a little scary, too, though, and reminded him of the dark places he had been in after the flood. He turned to go out, but he did not know which way out was. Then he saw a glimmer of light and heard familiar rattle. It was the jar of peanuts! Barbara was shaking the jar. He came running. He ate some peanuts, and purred and purred when she picked him up and carried him back inside the house.

Another day he slipped outside and went into the trees that were near the house. There were many things to sniff in there, but they were also sort of scary. When Barbara came outside and called him, he was glad to go to her. He thought that maybe exploring by himself was not something he wanted to do much of right now. When the winter was over and the weather was warm again, Barbara let him go outside, but she sat outside with him. She put the leash on his little harness and made sure he was tied up so he could not run into the woods or get into trouble.

When he got tired, his favorite place to take a

nap was curled up on Barbara's arm when she was working at her desk, with his head in the bend of her elbow. Or, he would put his paws around her neck, tuck his nose under her chin and purr, just as he had the first time they met at the shelter. She would stroke him and talk to him, even though the bigger he got, the harder it was to hold him there. "Some day you won't be able to do this," she told him, but he just purred louder, thinking that he would always do it. And he did keep doing it when he got bigger, and even though Barbara would say, "You're too heavy—you put my arm to sleep now," he would snuggle as close as he could and purr while she petted him.

Besides Raggedy and Princess, thousands of animals were rescued in those frightening weeks after the hurricanes and floods. Many were found by their people, and there were the happiest reunions you could imagine. But some, like Raggedy and Princess, went to new homes. Raggedy did not know it, but his picture was on the Internet along with pictures of hundreds of other animals, in case their owners ever had a chance to look for them. The day Barbara put his picture there, Raggedy was on the desk, watching the computer screen. She explained, "If your family looks for you here, you can go back to them. But if they don't, you will always have a home here."

Raggedy looked at the picture. He did not know it was him. All he could see was shapes, but he looked anyway, and batted his paw at the letters that were moving on the screen. "Does that mean you want me to take it off and you want to stay here?" Barbara asked him. He climbed onto her shoulder, put his paws around her neck and rubbed his nose on her chin. "Yes, I know—that's what got you here in the first place," she laughed, "your hugging and kissing routine." She hugged him back.

That night when they went to bed, Raggedy curled up close to Barbara. She heard him sigh in his sleep. In his dream, he was playing with a little girl, and he smiled and purred. He woke up just enough to think that this was a pretty good place to live, even if they did not know his name was Raggedy.

THE END

The Hurricane Katrina Animal Rescue

Some people left New Orleans before Hurricane Katrina, leaving enough food and water for a few days and telling their pets 'we'll be home soon'. Almost everyone else left the devastated city after the levees broke and the water flooded in, but they were not allowed to take their pets. Some people chose to stay with their pets and sadly some of them did not survive.

Thousands of animals were left on their own in the deserted city, locked in houses and roaming the streets. Pictures of the 'rooftop dogs' who found temporary safety on roofs of submerged houses filled the news. Outraged and compassionate animal lovers across the country converged on the area, to create the largest animal rescue effort ever done anywhere.

Hundreds of people spent hours and days and weeks risking their own health and safety combing the city looking for the animals that had been left behind. Hundreds more people worked day and night caring for the animals in the shelters where they were taken when rescued. Transports took the animals to all parts of the country and beyond.

No one left the experience untouched. Many fell in love with a rescued animal and went home with a new friend. Happily, there were reunions between people and their four legged friends.

This animal rescue and the nationwide coverage that it received helped lead to legislation ruling that whenever there is an evacuation, people must be allowed to take their pets away with them.

We pray that a disaster like this never happens again. We know that if it does, there are people who will step up and help.

Camp Katrina and HSLA

Camp Katrina is near Tylertown, Mississippi, about 90 miles north of New Orleans. The Humane Society of Louisiana, headquartered in New Orleans, had purchased the old farm property just a month before Hurricane Katrina, as a place to send animals rescued through their anti-cruelty work. After the storm the volunteers who found their way to this place on Obed-Magee Road had to create a shelter: building pens, repairing the small house, clearing land and so much more, while they rescued and cared for the animals.

Everyone worked from early morning to late at night, and then got up during the night to walk patrol around the property because people were trying to break in and steal dogs for dog fighting.

In a place where dozens of dogs were being sheltered, fed and walked every day, the 'Poop Can' was a very important thing!

Everyone worked and rested and laughed and cried together, and everyone made friends who will always be special because of what we shared. Everyone was there because they love animals and wanted to help. They did.

Camp Katrina is still in operation, caring for other rescued animals. HSLA is continuing its anti-cruelty and rescue work in and around New Orleans, in new quarters because their former home was lost in the floods.

The Hurricane Katrina Animal Memorial in

New Orleans honors the animals of the flood, and the people who saved so many of them.

Some Things about Streetcar

When I went to help at Camp Katrina, my friends teased me about how many animals I would bring back with me and I said none because I had two cats and that was fine. When Streetcar put his paws around my neck and kissed my chin I said 'Aw, shoot' because I knew that I would bring him home.

We estimated he was around five months old when he was rescued. That meant that a four month old kitten was able to survive for 32 days in the ruined city, without people, food, water or shelter. He was just one of many animals who made it through those hardships.

He was so skinny when he first got to Camp Katrina that you could see his ribs and his backbone. He is still slim. He also likes to eat just about anything. His favorite treat is peanuts. Other things he likes are peanut butter, asparagus, red jello with cool whip, and chicken.

He is fascinated by water. He really did sit in the bathroom and watch me take a shower the first night we stopped on the way home from Camp Katrina. He will come into the bathroom and sit on the edge of the tub and peek around the curtain when I am in the shower. He will also play with water coming out of the faucet, and he jumps into the tub when I get out, and licks the water around the drain.

When it is cold at night in the house, he will get under the covers in bed with me. He learned that from Mocha.

He likes to go outside, but I only let him out on a leash. Sometimes he sneaks out when I open the door, but then he will stop to eat grass so I can usually catch him right away.

His nicknames are Little Mister, Little Buddy and Brat Cat.

He still likes to put his paws around my neck and kiss my chin.

Other Katrina Rescue Stories, Websites and Related Things

- The Humane Society of Louisiana:
http://www.humanela.org/
- My experiences are at:
www.picturesandwordsbybarb.com
- There is a groups page that was started by and for Camp Katrina people and animals, now there are some Camp Katrina postings and also ones about other animal rescue:

    http://pets.groups.yahoo.com/group/CampKatrina4all4ever/

- A web site started by another Camp Katrina volunteer:

    http://www.campkatrina.net/

- There are several other books about the rescues. By doing a web search for Hurricane Katrina Animal Rescue you can get a list of many of them.

- "Dark Water Rising" is a documentary about

the animal rescues which focuses on a group who came to be known as Winn-Dixie, because they were set up in the parking lot of a Winn-Dixie supermarket. Because the film maker, Mike Shiley, went with rescue teams, much of it is very graphic; it is a true account of what the rescue work was like. I highly recommend it, but warn that it is very upsetting. I cannot watch it without crying.